This Coloring Book Belongs To

_____

DUFFY AND Duffy

All Rights Reserved
Duffy & Duffy Co
Copyright 2020
To contact the author
www.duffyandduffy.co

www.ingramcontent.com/pod-product-compliance
Lightning Source LLC
LaVergne TN
LVHW060858020325
804892LV00011B/347